GESTALT

poems

C. Show

new words {press}
A TRANS* & GENDER-EXPANSIVE POETRY PRESS

new words {press}
6030 Putnam Ave., New York, NY 11385
www.newwordspress.com | @newwordspress

new words {press} is a sponsored project of Fractured Atlas, a
non-profit arts service organization, with a mission of elevating
emerging and established trans* and gender-expansive poetic voices,
to build community, and share knowledge.

ISBN: 979-8-9903488-4-4

Cover design by C. Show
Typesetting by new words {press}

Printed in the United States of America

WHERE TO LOOK

For Papa Stephen. I promised I would dedicate my first book to you even though I knew you would never be able to read it. I will forever be ten years old, sitting on your green-topped cooler while you fish in the creek beside me.

Sprouting In Your Mouth

Violation is easy.

The red strikethrough cleaves sinew, ink spilling from the cut then
                              unname them for the   duration
        while a violet vein slithers rootlike   between you.   Pierce it.
        Harvest.
The reason for violence–to put them in their place   beneath
you   licking fury spins heat slick words   carving strokes deep
like gouges crunched into   inch-thick rind.
You've hurt   someone   before.   On purpose.

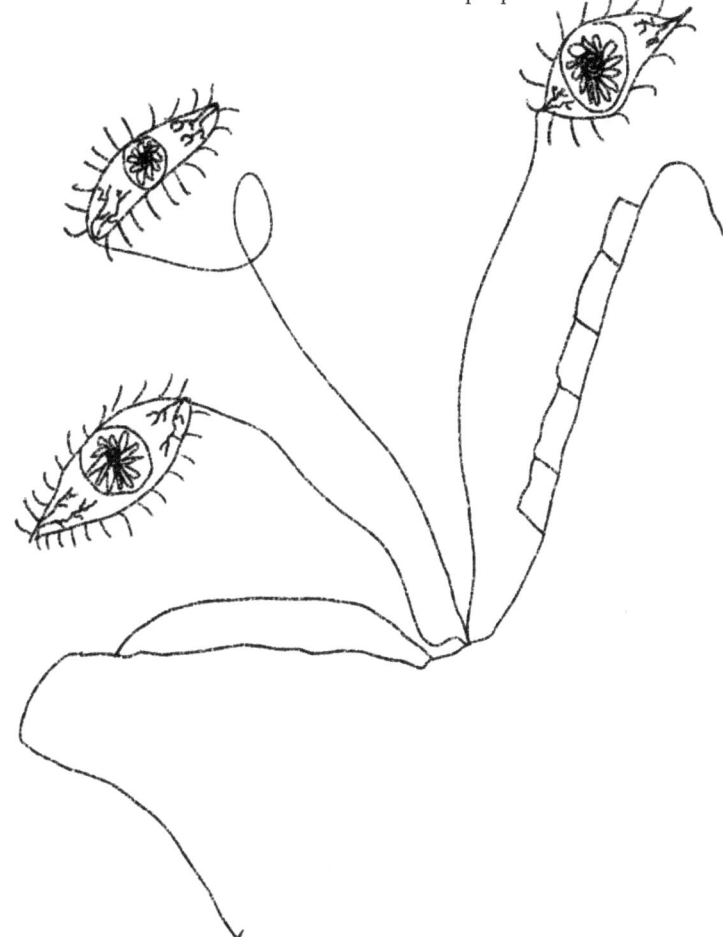

Constant Vigilance

Hugging edges I'm tiptoe   touching the ledge
            I'm extending it all   for hints of seismic quakes
                        that'll throw me over   falling.
            There's no warning   but if I'm still enough
                                    I feel it   the minutiae
                        stagnation
            dead wind and a yellow sky.
I'm silent   detecting   waiting to run
                                    if the water rises.
            Close bedroom door.   Lock it.
            Close bathroom door.   Lock it.
            Close door   to the toilet   and hide in the shower
                        as the tornado passes through.
            It's not supposed to hit us.   They don't go over hills
                                    and into valleys
                        but I hear the windows rattling.
            I'm struck
            sure I can stop the next one
                if I tread soft enough
                        but that has no bearing
                                    because
            no one ever told me kids don't control   the weather.

The Weight of It

I'm stuck
voice out
staring at the ceiling.   The jawed open abyss deeper than my fears
stretches past two bathroom doors   back further than
the tongue in my throat
gagging spit down my stomach.
Above I feel them watching me.
To the right, eyes.
An assault on all sides
I retreat inwards.   A bunker to shield (them) from (me)
a wrenched-tight cover curved crown-like.
This veil wards away evil
my chainmail against a blade.
Nothing slices   but a bruise forms under the skin.
Terror blooms a water   brown stain
in the ridges of assailant thumb prints
pressed against me like boots
soles   shaping themselves in my brain
the pattern of sharp tread bites.   Agony.
It's a long night to last. A long life too   suffering to what end
and   to whose enjoyment   save for
the makers of my misery.   There's no righteousness in this
no sainthood   waiting to swaddle me   in vestments.
Pain and what else?
I'm shrouded in makeshift armor.
Waiting.

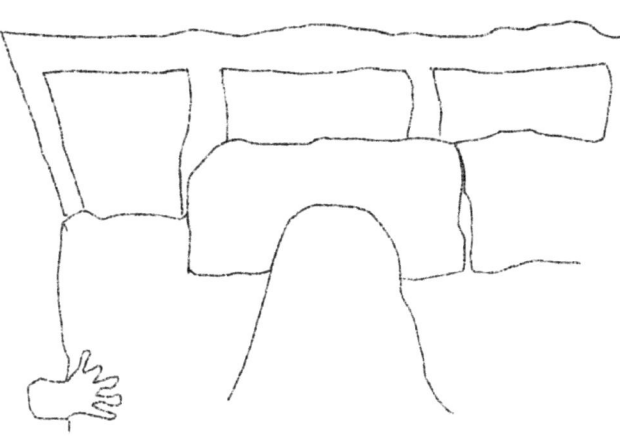

Helpless

No worse thing than a dead fish dream
gooey bodies suffocating while water soaks into the carpet.
I pick them up to deposit back in their tank
but the tank has disappeared.
Fish struggle
in the staggered pond– one side deep
the other a few centimeters.
I find myself hoping it's not too late.
A memory.
I'm 14 at the kitchen sink.
My blue beta fish drops to the cold metal
and I pick him up
afraid I've harmed him sure
he'll die immediately without my assistance.
In the dream my toes slip
over algae-greased rock
under the light of fluorescent bulbs
and the soft wet flesh of meter-long sturgeons
reminds me of the tales of catfish the size of buses
lurking in the lake right out of sight.
The sturgeons wade to shallow water
and when they find themselves beached on the kitchen floor
I try to carry them but
their bodies nearly fall apart
in my hands.
I know a fish has muscle
capable fins used to thrash and fight
and I've held a fish before
writhing from the hook
gauged in its cheek
but instead I imagine them
as waterlogged corpses dead skin
smushing off like my fingers in the bath.
"I can't keep doing this," I tell myself.
"I can't save them all."

Reaper's Bounty

Grubs in the sink turned flies in a day.
Dead overnight   then start again
        with hard brown seed-shaped
                    bodies stuck to metal and ceramic.
                        What's rotten?
What has died to attract them and breed   feeding on waste?
                    Show me
            and
                    I'll shove it to the bottom
                            of the bin where it will
                        fester   until trash day.
            Wriggling inside the sore   maggots eat full
                and transform into flies that
                    swarm my kitchen
                        reminders I can ignore   while their
                seeds sow themselves
                        out of sight until
        my house is a field at harvest.

Compulsion

A playing card flicks through
    the spokes of a
       bike at a clip
          quicker than
  movies ticking   their film reels away.
    My thoughts spin   with slides
          inserted between.   By who?
        Remember remember remember
    the bumps in the road   shake the car
and   quick zaps jolt at my temples
      the calm wrinkled   by the tail of a monster
                tip slicking a
                  wake before breach
                  a stick in the wheel
            now I'm crashing
      knee to pavement
    but the bike wheels   spin   stuck in place
      breathing smoke.   "Why have you stopped you're not done,"
                  I hear
      egging me back to my feet.
           "Put your hand in there. You have to,"
           it says.
        I cry.
     It kicked me off
      and   wants to shred my fingers
       as the rubber burns   through nothing left
              of the treads
  rims grinding out sparks on the street.

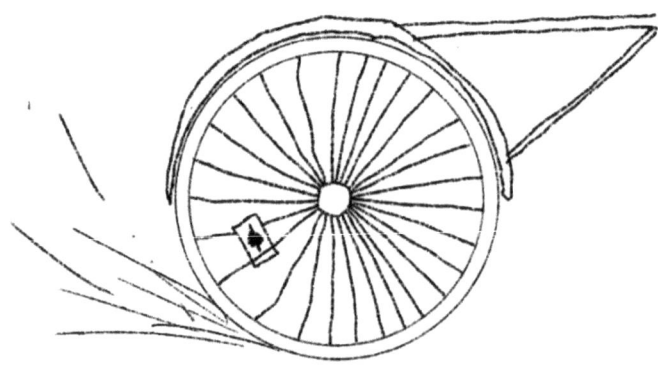

Collar

You're not alive.
Not in a way that matters.
They take you to a side room so they can lecture the others.

           You did nothing wrong.
           You did nothing.
       That's the point.
     To stay still.
      Bounce within the lattice-framed window
        waiting to hit a corner
        watching the dogs in the yard.
   It's getting dark   and
      they're still playing while
     you memorize what you've been told
    commands that keep
   you cocoon safe
  on the verge of something
    so thin a sheet to break
       but
   you're told the water's deep   and   hungry.
The dogs   collapse in a heap on the lawn
     a trio of content exhaustion
       hearts dropping to a lullaby
    rhythm
    and   you search
       for a reason they're wrong.

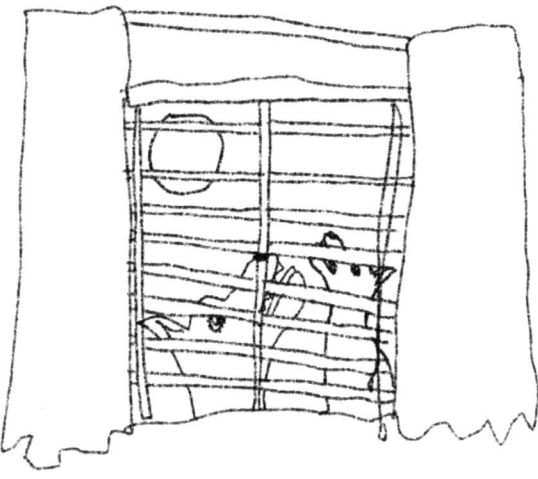

There Interposed

Don't feed me any affection.

I'll choke on it like a child.

Coughing it up

on the kitchen floor.

You'd think

I could stand it

the taste

the shape.

I spit it out

mistaking Kool-Aid for dish soap.

Peach rings for

fear.

Flesh

shrinks away from

the rind as your

skin grazes mine

and   it's

not   because you're filthy.

Sugar tastes bitter

when the taste buds are wrong.

You're doing it fine.

I'm the sick one.

Touch me   through the glass

so I won't be there when you do it.

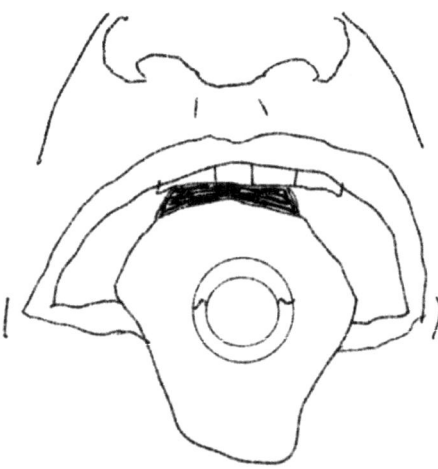

Closed Book

What if I'm scared?
They're on the verge   and
                    I stop.
Put it away   in the back of my closet
to pretend I've never touched.
                              Taking off her—
            and the next button
                              on the wheel
                  clicks away.
What's it like   to listen?
        I want to hear what happens.
                                    He watches her
                  so I watch her.
I close my eyes   because
            what's it like to see?
                        To see
                          and want.
Shove it away so I don't feel it.
                              Because
              what if I do   and nothing
                  is so real as my enjoyment.
They don't know to be ashamed
                        but I do.

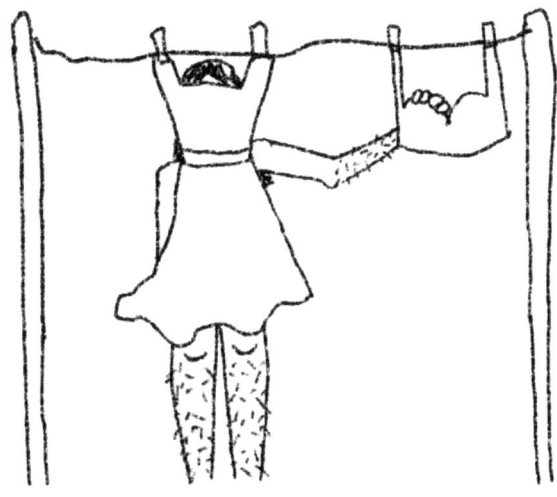

Consumption

To hollow out.
    A wasp in a fig   burrowing.
        You eat it.   What then?   Show me
    how you devour   others   and
          leave them walking.
      I fight   for space
    in my brain   you can't carve away
my words   too.   A colony
               of parasites
                   digging holes
              pinpricks
           where
        you come   and
         go   as you please.
      I'm not whole
        while you're here   and
        with you gone
     I'm empty.   The space in my
                  stomach that
        tells me
     I'm full   calls
  for your   presence   because
    without you   I've realized
                  reaching out for
         the missing
         mass that
       used to   writhe in
        my gut
      that I'm starving.   How do I eat
                    for myself?
      And can it grow back
-what you took?   A new body   I don't know   you
                      died   in me
                      digested   then spread
                     usurping.

Fruition

You're not relatable.   Balsamic tart stings their gums
        when they try to consume you.   Neutralize the acidity
                              and they'll
                swallow–
                        three segments transporting
                your taste   to an organ
                        poised to
                dissolve   you. Everyone's a connoisseur
                        prepared
                              to smell, swish, spit.
              What's an acceptable flavor?
                  Full-bodied.
                              Velvety.
                                      Opulent. You're
                jammy.
                                      Angular.
                        Idiosyncratic.
                                      Wrong barrel.
                                      Sour grapes.
                                      Plucked too
                        early and
                        forced   to ferment.
                        They wasted all these years
                to see how you'd turn out
          to see if you'd deliver.
"Toss the batch," they advise
and you beg
asking
"What can I change for you to stomach me?"

Net Worth

You were bad   but now you're good.

    Cross the line too many times, and you're bad again.

      The line is always in reach

        always in sight–

            a threat of what you might become

        or

            a taste of something better.

You tally up the times you've yelled

    to see how close you are   as the arrow clicks

      a few notches to the right.   The sum

           of all your actions equals your heart to be weighed.

           Every chance   you step on the scale

           to measure each fluctuation

  eyeing the feather-light impossible.

           If you inspect yourself enough

             shove your soul through

                a French press

          you'll shrink to a point

        deceptively small   and just as heavy

        a bowling ball thumbtack

           cracking the surface beneath.

       What's in it for scrutiny

          to condense you without change?

Pass you through a filter at least.

Siphon away the fumes   from the sulfur that burns inside

                until the smell's gone.

       It's not enough to be observed.

The reaction still has to take place.   The circumstances and the heat

              combined to make a product

              you can catalog

                to determine where you

        stand.

But the thing is it's always

      changing.

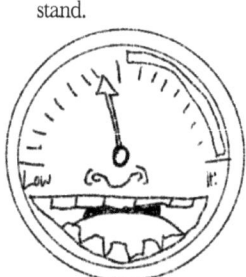

Feedback

I traipse through   swamp dense   thoughts thick
            as   sludge   sucking down
                                                waders to drown. The mind
                                    staggers
                                        wobbly
                                                            and
                                                        fractured
                            like an intricate toy
                                    like a part
                                            that's broken off
                                inside
                                                    and
                                        rattles around
                    when you shake it.
                    Head-sick
                            swimming
                                                        and
                                        weighed
                    like silver ball bearings   swishing
            ocean sounds   rolling   from the
scale   to the   counter   to the   floor.   Loose
    pellets spill   as   I pour   tinkling metal
            where the tray's supposed to be.
                                    Each scoop   bleeds
                                                as
                    I hold my position
                            willing   the wound to close.

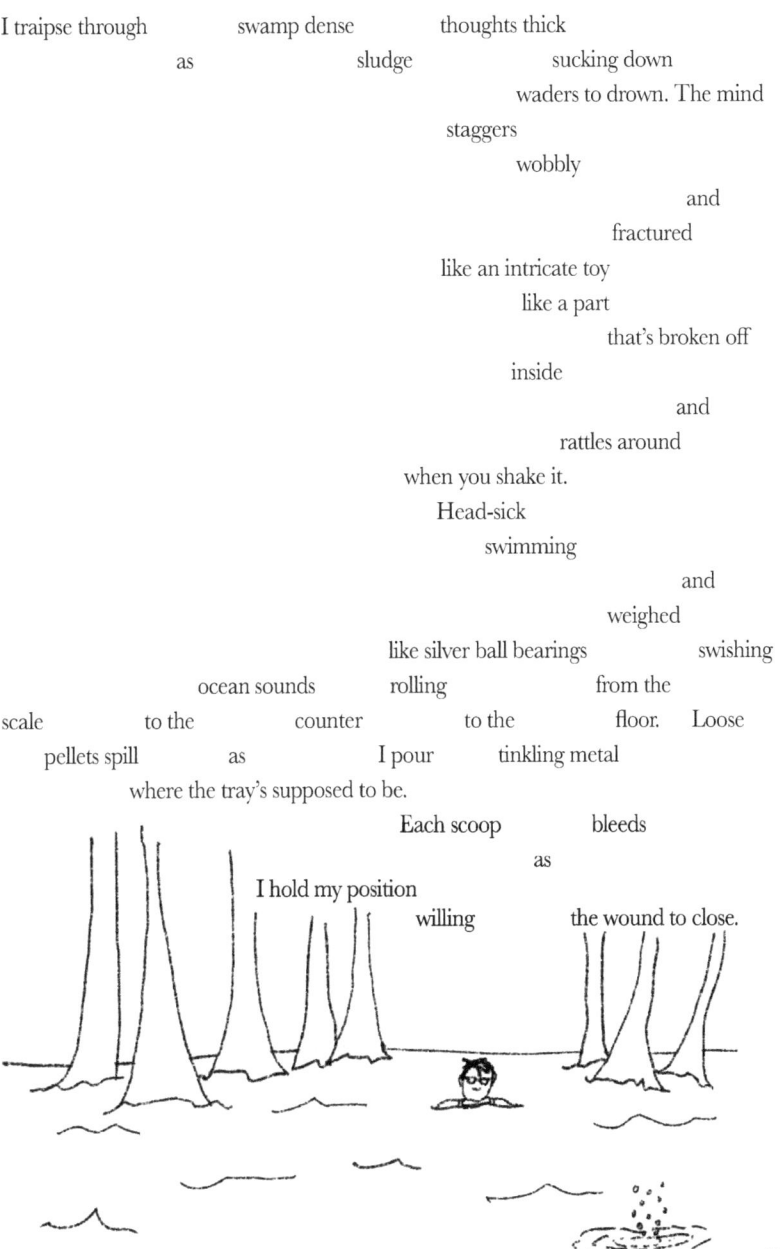

17

Tally Marks

The way you think–
    a razor lip-splitting
        skin in
        chicken scratch–
           that's   not the only way to hurt yourself.
                            Forearms dented by countertops
                                     pressing
                              your
                            weight
                      until the wedge imprints
                      upon you.
The cold as you drive
    one window down and
        an arm out freezing.
    You choose it   over stale lukewarm air meant to preserve.
The cold   like a burn you don't have to light
      instead   do nothing to change it.
        A passive harm is easier
               harder to keep track of.
      No countdowns or anniversaries   just a backslide
               roll down
        hanging in the breeze
night tasting your skin with its teeth.

Chronic

Static
elastic stretched
back too far to snap
back into shape.

Desecrated

polymer fibers
taxed beyond
tension to hang
warped and limp. They
drop down
my legs
when I   wear them.
When you   wear me
I slip off
caught dead on the street
willing my body   to move.
I'm silk   worn away   from
shoes on concrete   thin   like a hand-me-down shirt.
The fan   hums all the time
but   you can't survive without
stopping.

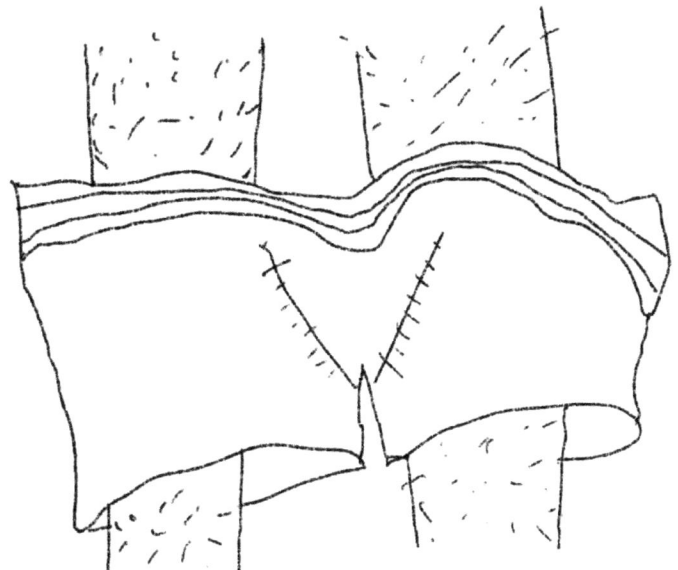

Breakthrough

Give way   the lock
                    clicks from
          a new measure
          something
                    borrowed
          from   another and
                    applied here.
          You wouldn't have
thought   but   now
                    the trunk   opens
                                        careful
                              in case
                         the lock
                    snaps
                    shut.   You
                              lay back
                              the lid
                                        gentle
                              with yourself
                    not used to   accessing
                              this unfamiliar   understanding
                         nascent   and   slow
                                             but   ready.

Open Maw

I just found out what it means to be   gentle.   Did you know how some
                    when surrounded by   sharp edges and violence   choose the soft bite?
Their teeth are   long and capable
but they work their jaws with grace   wolves   allowing the lamb to rest in
                    their mouths
                                                     in safety and peace   without bloodshed.
I have teeth   that cut   and a mind
                              that sharpens   blades whittling
                                             away the dead and   the
useless   like my great-great grandpa skinning his fingers
                                                     with his   pocket knife
                                             when pain and tension
                                             greet you as aunt and uncle
                                                     as friend and cousin–
          how are you to welcome what it means to be
          gentle?
          Is it true I was weaned on hate? I drank that insidious milk as though it
          were   love out of necessity,
                                                     out of
                                             hate's abundance
                                                           and when
                    presented with the real thing
I cannot tolerate it,
     do not trust it–

                                             though I crave the beautiful and
          true.
               Falsity
          and despair have overstayed their welcome in my bed.
          Those gentle
          jaws call to me   patiently
          waiting for me to lay my hand   inside

               and I must allow them to   close
                    on me with the force of a father's
                                   hand
               against the fragile
                         neck of his newborn child.

Steady

The plates chew   a jaw bone under the tides
                                   disturbing the water like talking
                                              like a voice in air.
        I'm unwell.   A tremor writhes through me
                    growing until it   registers from the deep
    and   I seize   threatening collapse.   The waves quake
                                              my eardrums.
                              Vertebrae rattles.
                         Processes shatter.
        My foundation wasn't built for this   and   my body
                                        rocks
                                   on a fulcrum
                              matching   the frequency.
Hold me.   Absorb it
until   the shock
passes   and I
return   fragile spun lacework pressed firm against the frame of your scaffold.

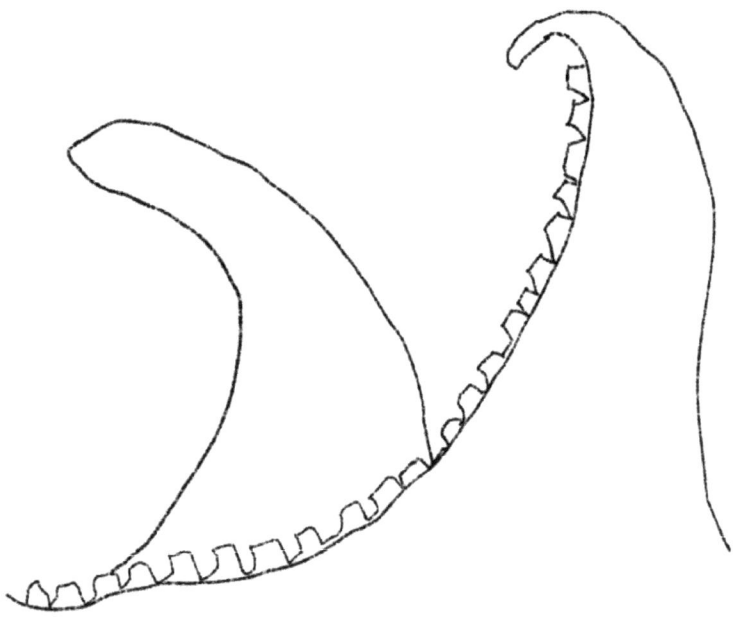

22

Aching Sound

It hurts when someone does it right
                              because
     then you know it's possible.   The failures mute
                                        the plucked string
                                     dampening the note
          but you hear it
                         like a fawn calling home.
                   You remember   what you're missing
          and   the presence makes the absence stronger
                                   the craving deeper
                    fresh legs stumbling   towards water
                              as the river pulls away
                    stretched back
                    like a rubber band
                                   after your first drink
                         or rather
                                        they could tug the stream closer
                         yet   they choose to let it run
                                                  ruts
                                   in the ground
                                   down a gorge
                                   out of reach.
                    Patience tries   and
                         ten years pass   so
                                   abandon
                                   your thistle-bound waiting.
                    Another source will find you
                              as long as you keep on asking.

23

Firmament

Why is it sharp?
    The diamond head
        drill bits
       studding my mind bore
           holes as I think.
      Razor wire   lines the walls and
             drags deep   as I struggle.
     This is on reflex.   A self-taught pain.
        I instruct the points to soften
               spikes melting to a
                   calm blue pool
                   a wing soft bed.
  It's a conscious thing   love.
  It's an effort or else   to stick my hand   inside
        and   feel my teeth sink down from habit.
    The harm is a distraction   static blurring the message
          or else
        I'll hear it
           that empty nothing.
      Scrub the cobweb
        cracks
     spiraling toward the
       center   and leave
    that nothing   room
    to echo whatever
      wanders inside.
    No
    not
    nothing   color and sound
        a starry gradient
        dotting the walls with
        synth string accompaniment
          caressing
    blood   and   brain   and   bone.
Your world doesn't have to be empty   but
    it doesn't have to hurt.

About the Author

C. Show (they/them) is a Central Arkansan poet and writer who finds safety in the speculative, in satire, and in experimental poetic forms. They are always working on a piece whether that be a poem, a zine, a short story, a play, a novel, or an essay. This variety allows them the freedom to express themself and to stretch their creativity when they've overexerted themself in one outlet. The format of their poems in Gestalt stems from their experience with synesthesia wherein sight and physical sensation are crossed. The scattered words and phrases create the feeling of a rainstorm of droplets and evoke the metal cylinder of a music box, plucking the strings of meaning with each turn. Their short fiction has been previously published in *ImageOutWrite*, *Flash Fiction Magazine*, and *Every Day Fiction*. You can follow their work on Instagram @_cshow_.